THEN & NOW
NUTLEY

This is the home of Thomas W. Satterthwaite. His property extended from approximately Grant Avenue north to Kingsland Street and from the Passaic River west to Passaic Avenue. The Satterthwaite estate was known as Nutley. The name was derived from *Nut,* for all the nut trees on the estate, and the English word *ley,* meaning a tract of open land, a field, or a meadow. Therefore, the definition of the word *Nutley* is a field of nut trees.

THEN & NOW
NUTLEY

Marilyn Peters and Richard O'Connor

ARCADIA
PUBLISHING

Published by Arcadia Publishing
Charleston, South Carolina

Printed in the United States of America

Library of Congress Catalog Card Number: 2002108569

For all general information contact Arcadia Publishing at:
Telephone 843-853-2070
Fax 843-853-0044
E-mail sales@arcadiapublishing.com
For customer service and orders:
Toll-Free 1-888-313-2665

Visit us on the Internet at www.arcadiapublishing.com

*To my husband, Tom, and my daughters Heather and Tracy Ann.
Their love and support inspire me to be all I can be. To my coauthor, Rich,
who knows that through adversity comes strength.*

—Marilyn Peters

*To my wife, Donna, and son Sean for all their love, support, patience,
and understanding. To my coauthor, Marilyn—you know that
when a door closes, a window opens.*

—Richard O'Connor

CONTENTS

ACKNOWLEDGMENTS

The authors would like to thank the Nutley Historical Society and its board of directors for their willingness to help in making this project possible. The Nutley Museum has a wealth of information about the past residents and the history of Nutley. The building that the society and museum are housed in is a part of that history, and it awaits visitors to educate them about all the treasures that it holds.

When this undertaking began, many people came forward to offer photographs and factual information about the history of Nutley. This assistance was given freely and with a great sense of pride in their community. Nutley has always been and continues to be a community that many towns try to replicate, but few ever succeed. It is with sincere appreciation that thanks are given to the Nutley Historical Society; Joseph's Photographers and Stanley Fejnas; Fred and Jeanne Van Steen; Anthony Andriola; Barry Simone; Mario Gaetano; Fran Bouton; Mayor Peter Scarpelli; Commissioner Carmen Orechio; Commissioner Joanne Cocchiola; Commissioner Mauro Tucci; Fire Chief Tom Peters and Deputy Fire Chief Fred Scalera; the members of the Nutley Fire Department; Ed Stecewicz; Vincent LoCurcio III; Nutley High School, including Joseph Zarra, Terri Verdi, Angelo Frannicola, and Matt Mairella; the Nutley Board of Education, including Dr. Kathleen Serafino and Katherine Mulligan; Rev. Jill Fenske; Sean O'Connor, Eric Scalera, Alexis Gerst-Peters, Mikey Peters, Nick Bucci, Steve Lotito, Katie Marano, Matt Marano, Christopher Panzera, Joey Panzera, and Mike Tibaldo; Tracy Ann Peters; Heather Chadwick; Donna O'Connor; Gary and Donna Korkula; Fr. David Hubba of St. Mary's Church; Fr. Thomas J. Ciba of Our Lady of Mount Carmel Church; and the members of the Nutley Volunteer Emergency Rescue Squad.

INTRODUCTION

The township of Nutley is a small community located in Essex County, New Jersey. It has a rich history and preserves its sense of community even today.

The history of Nutley dates back to 1666, when Capt. Robert Treat purchased the whole valley from the Passaic River to the Watchung Mountains and from Newark Bay to the Yountakah River from the Native Americans. This new area was called Newark. Nutley, as the area would eventually be called, was heavily wooded except for the land near the Passaic River. While the earliest English settlers made their homes along the Passaic River, the Dutch moved farther inland and cut their farms out of the forest.

The Newark Schedules were surveys that stated ownership of the land. The Vreeland estate is the only Dutch-owned property recognized in the Newark Schedules. According to the documents, in 1702, it was owned by Jacob Vreeland. During the American Revolution, the estate was confiscated, and, when the war ended, Capt. Abram Speer claimed it as his own. He sold it to John M. Vreeland, Jacob's grandson, in 1783. It remained in the Vreeland family until the early 1900s, when the Woman's Club of Nutley took on the task to preserve the building. This historical building has survived for 300 years and is still the home of the Woman's Club of Nutley.

Boundary changes would begin to occur when the Bloomfield section, which included the areas that would eventually become Belleville and Nutley, seceded from Newark in 1812. In 1839, Belleville, which included Franklin, broke away from Bloomfield, feeling that they were not being fairly represented by the local government. In 1874, for much the same reason, Franklin, measuring only a little over three square miles, separated itself from Belleville. Finally, on March 5, 1902, Franklin chose to change its name to Nutley.

In the latter part of the 19th century, Franklin was a weekend retreat for many New Yorkers and was home to many artists and writers of the time. It was here that Henry Cuyler Bunner, editor of *Puck* magazine, which was one of the three leading magazines of that time, decided to reside. Bunner's home was quite large, and he entertained many guests. One frequent visitor to his home was Mark Twain, who wrote articles for *Puck* and was a good friend of Bunner. Another frequent visitor to town was Annie Oakley. She and her husband, Frank Butler, were so taken with the town that they purchased property on Grant Avenue and built a home there, where they resided for several years.

During the 1890s, plans were made for a trolley to run through the town to make local commuting faster and easier. The largest stumbling block was whether the tracks should be laid along Passaic Avenue, where the business district made its home. Wealthy homeowners in that area preferred not having trolley tracks so near to their homes and lobbied to have them put farther west instead. In the mid-1890s, trolley tracks were laid along Franklin Avenue, which at the time was a mostly residential area. With the convenience of the trolley and the West Nutley Train Station located on High Street, the business district soon relocated to Franklin Avenue, and it became the center of town. Many of the homes along Franklin Avenue were converted to businesses, and some were replaced by more commercial structures.

During this time of expansion in the early 1900s, the town realized the need to preserve some of the land as parkland. While the issue was being discussed with the county, part of the property where the Duncan Mills had been located, which is now Vincent Place, was sold to the Methodist Church and the Bank of Nutley. This prompted officials to act quickly and designate the remaining property as parkland. Nutley's efforts to maintain open areas continued, and it now contains more than 125 acres of parkland.

During the late 1800s and early 1900s, several of the large estates were sold to developers, such as William Lambert, who was an architect, builder, and president of Nutley Realty Company. Lambert built approximately 500 homes in Nutley, as well as commercial and municipal buildings. Although Nutley's population of approximately 5,000 continued to grow rapidly and the number of houses increased, the town retained its sense of community. Many of the original buildings are still in use as homes and businesses today.

Today, with a population of approximately 28,000 residents, Nutley still maintains a unique small-town feeling throughout its quiet, well-maintained tree-lined streets. As you will see as you go through this book, many of the original buildings look much the same as they did 100 years ago or more. We are very proud of our rich heritage, and we strive to preserve it for generations to come.

Meadowside was the part of the Satterthwaite estate where Larkin House stood in 1890. When the estate was divided and sold in 1922, the property was taken over by the Yountakah Country Club, and Larkin House became the clubhouse. A few years later, a fire destroyed the house and another clubhouse was built in its place. In 1943, ITT purchased the property and occupied it until 1995, when it was sold to Town and Country Developers for the construction of Cambridge Heights.

Chapter 1

HOMES AND STREETS

A llan Stirratt was a liveryman and horseman. He owned the livery stable on Chestnut Street where the Nutley Volunteer Emergency Rescue Squad now has its quarters. For years, he provided horses and carriages to the gentlemen of Nutley. He had regular customers who booked a horse once or twice a week to go courting. Stirratt also had sleighs for hire so that courting would not be interrupted in the winter months when snow was too deep. Shown here are Allan Stirratt, his daughter Eleanore (in the hat), and Eleanore's friend Grace. The house behind them is located at 22 Beech Street. As you can see, the integrity of this well-maintained home has been kept, and structurally it looks much the same as it did when the photograph of the Stirratts was taken in 1915.

Jacob Vreeland built the Vreeland House, located at 226 Chestnut Street, in 1702. At the close of the Revolutionary War, the estate was confiscated. After the war ended, Capt. Abram Speer purchased the property. He sold the house and part of the land to John M. Vreeland. It remained in the Vreeland family until the early 1900s. Tenants who occupied the house at that time allowed the property to fall into a state of disrepair. In 1912, a group of civic-minded women who were organizing themselves into the Woman's Club of Nutley took on the task of preserving the Vreeland House as a historical landmark. The house was restored and remains the Woman's Club of Nutley to this day.

This house was built by William R. Sergeant for his wife, Edith Leaman Sergeant, and their family. Their daughter Maud Frances married John Vernou Bouvier Jr., and they eventually became the grandparents of Jacqueline Bouvier Kennedy. As a child, Jacqueline came to Nutley with her parents to visit her great uncle Edgar Sergeant. She was quoted as saying, "I have never lived there, just driven through the town as a little girl, with my father pointing out things to me. . . . A pond where he went ice skating is what I remember most."

That pond is known as the Mud Hole, where residents still ice-skate in the winter months. In 2001, the Sergeant house was sold to a developer who had planned to demolish it and replace it with several upscale modern homes. Due to the efforts of several neighbors and the Nutley Historical Society backing the preservation of historic buildings within the town, the developer abandoned his plans and sold the house and property to buyers who wished to restore and live in the house.

William A. Lambert was an architect and builder in Nutley during the late 1800s and early 1900s. His designs were in good taste with the flavor of his native England. The home on the left in the picture below is the one he designed and built for him and his family. Lambert bought much of the Satterthwaite estate and built more than 100 houses there. He also bought several parcels of land on what are now Hillside Avenue, Prospect Street, Sylvan Place, Daily Street, and Raymond Avenue for $200 an acre, and he proceeded to build hundreds more homes. His first 6-room homes sold for $3,600 to $4,000. Later, he began building 8- and 10-room homes for $5,000 to $5,500, and even a few 12-room homes that he sold for $6,000. He and a partner went into business as the Nutley Realty Company to sell his creations. By the end of his career, he had built more than 500 homes in Nutley and other buildings, including the West Nutley Train Station and the firehouse on High Street.

13

The Kingsland Manor was built c. 1750. Joseph Kingsland Sr. purchased the home at a sheriff's sale in the 1790s and moved into the house with five of his nine children. Joseph Kingsland Jr. inherited the house, and his two daughters lived there until 1902. The property was sold in 1909 and, between then and 1938, it was used as a training camp for prizefighters, a speakeasy, a legal club after Prohibition, a convalescent home, and then a private home. The township of Nutley purchased it in 1973 in an effort to preserve this significant part of Nutley's history.

Annie Oakley and her husband, Frank Butler, purchased the property located at 302-306 Grant Avenue in 1892. They built their house at 304 Grant Avenue and lived there for several years. It was said that the house was built without thought to closets, as for years Oakley had lived out of trunks. Oakley took an active part in the social life of Nutley. She put on exhibitions and participated in the Nutley Circus held in the Eaton Stone training ring on Kingsland Street, where Hoffmann La Roche is now located, for the benefit of the first Red Cross Fund. The property was sold to Joseph Stirrattt in 1904, when Oakley decided she wanted to return to touring sharpshooting exhibitions. Later, it was sold again to a developer, and the house, which stood directly in the center of the property, was demolished on August 16, 1937, to make room for two modern brick homes.

The Four Maples was built by John Bradbury in the early 1700s. His grandson John Abraham Van Riper put a large addition on the house when he wed Leah Winne in 1776. The house remained in the family until 1883. It changed hands several times after that and finally became the property of ITT in 1943. The property was sold to Town and Country Developers in 1995, and the Van Riper house would have been demolished had it not been for a concerted effort by Nutley citizens to preserve this important piece of history. Town and Country Developers subsequently donated the house and the immediate surrounding property to the township of Nutley and, at present, the Van Riper house is being restored.

This is the corner of Hillside Avenue and High Street. In the early 1900s, it became a very popular area due to the High Street Railroad Station directly across the street, which made commuting to and from New York City very convenient. A half block east of this corner was one of the Great Atlantic & Pacific Tea Company locations. It was only one block from Franklin Avenue, where many businesses were located and where the trolley ran for more local commutes. All these amenities made this area particularly desirable.

This is a view of the houses located at 661 and 665 Franklin Avenue in 1895. During that time, Franklin Avenue was a mostly residential area. When what was known as the center of town moved from Passaic Avenue and Chestnut Street down to Franklin Avenue, the area slowly became more commercial rather than residential. Some of the homes, such as the ones shown here, survived the transition and were converted to offices, but many were torn down and replaced with commercial buildings.

E.P. Cook and his family lived in this home, located at 145 Centre Street. The back of this photograph, dated 1910, states that the people shown are Virginia and Melvin, but no last name is mentioned. The house has been well preserved and visually remains unchanged.

This view of Highfield Lane shows two historic buildings. The first building on the left was Connolly's Meat Market. It also contained a hall where political rallies were held. The second building on the left is Guthrie's Store, which was built in 1894 and designed by a New York architect. Guthrie's was a gathering place for many residents and visitors. Annie Oakley and Mark Twain visited the store often to enjoy the homemade ice cream and use the telephone booth that was located there. The telephone booth, as well as many other artifacts from Guthrie's, is now on display in the Nutley Museum at 65 Church Street. Edmund J. Guthrie and his sister May closed the store in the 1940s, rebuilt the front, and substituted a residential entrance.

During the late 1800s and early 1900s, this home, at 192 Nutley Avenue, was very desirable. Not only was it a large comfortable home on a large piece of property, but its location, only a few blocks southeast of the railroad station and a few blocks west of the Passaic River (two major means of transportation), made homes such as this much sought after.

This house, shown above *c.* 1895, is located at 653 Franklin Avenue. It is one of the homes that survived the transition when Franklin Avenue became the center of town and changed from being a residential area to a commercial area. The house was eventually converted into the offices of Dr. Bruce Ollins, an orthodontist who, when refurbishing the building, did a wonderful job of preserving the architectural integrity of the original structure.

These three houses are located on Centre Street. The house on the left is No. 61, and the house in the center is No. 69. Both were built *c.* 1890. The house on the right of the picture was built in the early 1900s. All three of these homes were built by Peter Yereance.

At one time, the Woodruff House, built *c.* 1840, was a store. Shown above *c.* 1889 are, from left to right, James Woodruff, who was born in the homestead in August 1859; his three sisters; his father, Johnathon Woodruff; and an unidentified man. The property had a 100-foot-deep well that provided sparkling clear water and brought neighbors from near and far to avail themselves of the refreshing well water. Anthony Rich purchased the property in 1920, but wishing to retain the rights to the well, James Woodruff made a stipulation in the deed that allowed him to secure water from the well at his discretion. The arrangement proved unsatisfactory to both parties, and, finally, Woodruff relinquished his water rights for the sum of $1,000.

The Grace Church rectory is located at 204 Highfield Lane. When Rev. John P. Appleton arrived in Franklin in 1890, with his wife and six children, to take on the duties of the permanent rector of Grace Church, there was no rectory to house them. A rented home for them to reside in proved very costly to the church. In September 1891, the Satterthwaite family donated a parcel of land located at the corner of Highfield Lane and North Road for the purpose of building a rectory. In January 1892, plans were drawn and accepted. It was built by Henry M. Whitfield in the New England Queen Anne style originating from the Georgian style of the 1700s. The rectory was dedicated in 1893, having cost $6,850 to build.

Located at 197 Nutley Avenue, Woodcroft was built in 1895 by John Vernou Bouvier Jr., a well-respected New York lawyer. He married Maud Frances Sergeant, and they had a son, John III, and twin daughters, Maude and Michelle. He made and lost millions of dollars in the stock market and became known as Blackjack Bouvier. He was very active in Nutley's affairs, serving as president of the Nutley Field Club, a trustee at St. Mary's Church, president of the board of education, and director of the Bank of Nutley. In 1906, he was the Democratic candidate for councilman in the Third Ward. John III married Janet Lee in 1928, and their daughter Jacqueline would, on September 12, 1953, become the wife of John Fitzgerald Kennedy.

Henry M. Whitfield once owned this home, located at 131 Brookfield Avenue. Whitfield built many of the houses in the Erie Place district. In 1893, he was also responsible for building the Grace Episcopal Church rectory, located at 204 Highfield Lane.

Residence of J. R. Hay, Built in 1800, Nutley, N.

Located at 385 Passaic Avenue, this house was originally built by John Mason in 1812. In later years, it was the home of James R. Hay, a real estate developer in town. Hay was very active in community affairs in Nutley; he was one of the founding fathers and one of the first vestrymen of the newly organized Grace Episcopal Church in October 1873. The property on either side of the long driveway was later developed and is now Calico Lane. Hay's house can still be found at the end of that street.

In 1769, Capt. Abram Speer built this house, located at 149 Church Street, as a dowry for his wife, Emmetche Wouters. A tiny one-room stone building was constructed close to the main house to serve as a kitchen. The loft over the kitchen was used as quarters for the family slave, Nancy. After his death in 1834, the last two remaining slaves in Nutley belonging to Captain Speer were freed. Captain Speer had four daughters, and the property remained in the family through one of them who married John Stager. In turn, their daughter Dorcas married Daniel Pake. Dorcas and Daniel Pake's daughter Sarah later married Daniel Tuers, and the property remained in the Tuers family until it was sold in 1929.

Between 1871 and 1890, James R. Hay built a cluster of 11 wooden cottages on Erie Place to house United States Express employees who were under exclusive contract with the Erie Railroad. The identical homes each contained four rooms and have been described as Folk Victorian. Hay played a significant role in the development of the town. He was one of the founding fathers of an Episcopal Church in Franklin, founded the town's first water system, and was involved in changing the town's name from Franklin to Nutley. Hay's significance to the town, as well as the vintage homes and their connection to the railroad, made it possible for the street to attain historical status in 1993, and it is now known as the Erie Place Historic District.

This was Thomas J. O'Neil's home, located at 142 Brookfield Avenue. O'Neil served as one of the officers for the George La Monte & Son Paper Company. His son Thomas Jr. and grandson Thomas O'Neil Moore also worked for the company. George La Monte held the patent for National Safety Paper, which became a significant and necessary part of the banking business. O'Neil was very active in town affairs and was the Democratic candidate for mayor in 1906.

During the town's early stages of home developments in the late 1800s, houses such as these on Maple Place were beginning to be built as large estates were sold and subdivided. Behind these houses, in the distance, the Erie Railroad tracks can be seen. If you were to travel a few blocks east of Maple Place, you would have found the Nutley Train Station, located on Highfield Lane and Whitford Avenue. Because of the close proximity to rail transportation, this was a very desirable area to own a home.

During the late 1800s, this home was located at the northeast corner of Franklin Avenue and Centre Street. As this area of town became more commercial, many of the private residences were converted into businesses or demolished so that commercial buildings could be built. Most of the commercial buildings that replaced the one-family homes were built with apartments on the second and third floors, thus allowing the residents the convenience of living in the center of town.

Many one-family homes could be seen along Franklin Avenue during the late 1800s and early 1900s, but as the business district relocated itself from Passaic Avenue and Chestnut Street to Franklin Avenue, more and more homes were demolished to make way for commercial buildings. This house was located on the southwest corner of Franklin Avenue and Church Street across from the Park School (now the Nutley High School). If you look to right in the current view of this corner, you will see Franklin Reformed church at the top of the hill on Church Street.

The Mile Stretch was well known to Nutley residents in the early 1900s. From Kingsland Street in front of the Feurerbach Hotel to the finish line at Michael Gorman's tavern at Grant Avenue, Washington Avenue became a racetrack every Sunday and on holidays when gentlemen drivers would come from miles to race their trotters. Joe Stirratt and his champion horse Frontier took on many challengers in the weekly trotting and pacing races. The races also attracted many famous personalities, including Annie Oakley and her husband, Frank Butler; Mark Twain; and Henry Cuyler Bunner, editor of *Puck* magazine.

The Dodd House, located at 90 Vreeland Avenue, was among the houses built in the early 1800s. The property on which the house was located reached beyond the Erie Railroad. It was purchased by John T. Dodd on July 5, 1828, from John V. Brown, his wife, Keziah Brown, and his sister, Leah Brown. John Dodd had only one son, James, who produced five children by his first wife, Elizabeth F. Long. Their son Joshua was killed in the Civil War. Elizabeth died in 1847, and James remarried Gemima, who died in 1849 along with their child. He was married a third time to Angelina, who also died with child in 1853. A fourth marriage, to Mary, produced five children—three sons and two daughters. The three sons, Thomas Wesley, Franklin M., and William H., all left to live in New Zealand. Dodd died on October 30, 1879, and is buried in the Methodist cemetery on Passaic Avenue. His two unmarried daughters, Jennie E. and Anna M., continued to live in the family homestead for many more years.

One hundred years ago, this area of town was a very popular place to reside. These pictures show Whitford Avenue in a view looking north from Grant Avenue. In the early 20th century, Grace Episcopal Church would have been where the white home in the picture to the right now stands; Annie Oakley's house would have been only a few houses to the west along Grant Avenue. If you traveled north a few blocks, you would find the Nutley Train Station. It was indeed a very desirable area in which to own a home.

In the late 1800s and early 1900s, William Lambert built many of the homes in this area of town known as Nutley Park. These pictures show the northwest corner of Whitford and Brookfield Avenues. The large house on the corner still remains and looks very much the same as it did 100 years ago.

This picture shows the Nutley Outlet Sewer Tunnel on the day that the final blast broke through the tunnel on November 3, 1920. Commissioner Schaff was given the honor of throwing the switch that set off the last blast. Afterward, the entire group walked through the tunnel from the abandoned quarry, under Washington Avenue, to a point on the grounds of the Yountakah Country Club.

Chapter 2

PUBLIC SAFETY
AND THE
MUNICIPALITY

In the late 1800s, Dr. A. Harvey Van Riper petitioned the town to form a fire company. Yantacaw Hose and Truck Company was formed on March 5, 1894, with Dr. Van Riper as the department's first fire chief. The fire department was housed in the left side of the town hall and, during the first year, had an operating budget of $1,000. On November 6, 1894, the first piece of equipment, a hand-drawn chemical engine and wagon, was purchased at a cost of $1,250. The wagon was meant to be drawn by firemen but turned out to be too heavy and was altered to be pulled by horses.

Put into service in 1897, this hose cart was purchased from East Orange by Dr. A. Harvey Van Riper, the first chief of the fire department, when the town was still known as Franklin. After more modern firefighting apparatus had replaced it, the hose cart was stored at the High Street firehouse. Later, it was moved to the Nutley Museum and put on display. In the late 1960s, a group of volunteer firefighters in town decided to take on the daunting task of restoring this wonderful piece of fire department history. The hose cart was completely disassembled and lovingly restored to its original glory. In 1988, it was presented at the New Jersey State Firemen's Convention in Wildwood, where it won first prize. It is now on loan to the Firemen's Home in Boonton, where it is proudly displayed in their museum.

Avondale Hook and Ladder Company No. 1 became the town's second fire company in December 1894. They were officially recognized by the township as a bucket brigade on April 5, 1895. They would not be called to duty until June, when they responded to Miller's hut in the woods. Company No. 1 soon realized that in the future, they would need more than buckets to fight a substantial fire and accepted the town's offer to use the hose cart until such time that they were able to acquire a hook-and-ladder truck. They met at the home of Wright Sutcliff until September 1, 1898, when they moved into their new headquarters on Avondale Road (now Park Avenue) near the corner of Weston Street. At the November 1898 meeting, the members voted to change their name to Avondale Hose Company No. 1. In 1905, a new combination chemical engine, hose carriage, and hook and ladder were acquired. In that same year, the firemen requested that the company be given $400 per year out of which each fireman would be paid $2 for each fire they attended, with the balance of the money reverting to the company at the end of the year. This request was denied and instead, in January 1906, the town council approved the payment of $12 per year to each fireman.

On February 13, 1906, a group of citizens gathered together to draft a letter to Harry Stager, the fire chief, requesting a fire company be established to protect the northwest section of the town. The town council approved the establishment of the West Nutley Hose Company No. 2 at its meeting on March 14, 1906. It was decided that the new firehouse would be located at 200 High Street, and the architect and builder would be William Lambert. Upon completion, the hose cart from Avondale Hose Company No. 1 was transferred to the new firehouse. The company was paid $7 per month for the upkeep of the horses that pulled the hose cart, and the firefighters were paid $12 per year for their services. Today, if a volunteer firefighter makes a quota of at least 60 percent of all alarms, he or she is paid approximately 55¢ per day or a maximum of $200 per year as a clothing allowance

stipend. These dedicated men and women risk their lives protecting the life and property of the citizens of Nutley out of an extreme sense of duty and certainly not for the monetary compensation.

The Nutley Public Safety Building, located at 228 Chestnut Street, was built in 1929 and dedicated on Memorial Day 1930. Previously located in the town hall building, the fire and police departments were growing in members and equipment. The new public safety building provided enough space to include not only essential services but the municipal court as well. Within the past few years, the courtroom has been used for the filming of the television show *Ed*.

Originally built as a mill in the 1800s, the town hall, located at 1 Kennedy Drive, has undergone many changes. On February 8, 1904, a fire destroyed the roof of the building. During reconstruction, a third floor was added, and the police and fire departments were headquartered there until 1929, when a new public safety building was built at 228 Chestnut Street. The building became the official town hall in 1952 and remains so today. In recent years, because of his outstanding service and dedication to the township of Nutley, the building was renamed the Harry W. Chenoweth Municipal Building.

The photograph above, taken on November 13, 1914, shows the members of Nutley's first town commission. Shown seated, from left to right, are Henry T. Lefferts, Mayor Abram Blum, and Arthur R. Carr. Behind them are the members of the fire department. Shown seated in the current picture, from left to right, are Joanne Cocchiola, Nutley's first female commissioner; Mayor Peter Scarpelli; Commissioner Carmen Orechio; and department chaplain Fr. Thomas J. Ciba. Those standing are members of Hose Company No 2, Hose Company No. 1, Yantacaw Company, Headquarters Company, and fire department secretaries Mary Mosca and Mary Ann Romas. Shown standing in the front row between the two officers in white hats is Tracy Ann Peters, who is the first female fire officer in the Nutley Fire Department. Currently, the fire department has 102 firefighters, 5 engines, a truck, a foam truck, and an alarm truck. Nutley also has 3 hazardous materials trucks and a team of hazardous materials technicians that serve all of Essex County, excluding Newark.

Prior to the organization of the Nutley Police Department, residents had only chancemen and constables to protect the town. A series of robberies in which 16 homes were burglarized in one evening led to the town's decision to fund the cost of a regular police department. In 1910, a paid force of five men were put into operation. Police headquarters was located in the town hall, where the town's first jail, a steel cage, was located. The officers were paid $50 per month, with one day off every two weeks, and covered the day in two shifts. They walked an average of 12 miles per day and covered the entire town. Other than their nightsticks and .32-caliber revolvers, they had no equipment. The police department had no patrol wagon, so if a call came in, the officers would flag down the first vehicle that passed and commandeer it for use. The problem was, however, that in those days, traffic was not all that heavy and they never knew how long they would have to wait for someone to come by. In 1911, the police acquired their first vehicle, a combination ambulance and patrol wagon pulled by a team of horses. Today, the

Nutley Police Department consists of 66 officers and approximately 30 vehicles, in addition to other specialized equipment for aiding and protecting the public. The four officers above are, from left to right, Robert Irwin, Anthony Montanari, Sgt. Gail Ferrara (Nutley's first female police officer), and Thomas Schenke.

The Nutley Library moved into its new location at 381 Passaic Avenue in August 1904. The annual subscription fee for the privilege of borrowing books was $3. After residents voted to have a free public library in November 1912, the trustees of the Nutley Library decided to close its doors on January 1, 1914, and donated approximately 3,000 books to the new library. The building was sold and is now a private home.

On November 11, 1912, Mayor Abram Blum appointed the first board of trustees of the Free Public Library of Nutley. Since no money was available at the time, the first year was devoted to planning for the library. In April 1913, $20,000 was received from the Carnegie Corporation. On May 6, 1913, the citizens of the school district voted to donate the triangular piece of land between Booth Drive, Vincent Place, and the Park School for the construction of the new library. Later in May, Armstrong and DeGelleke of New York were engaged as the architects for the building. In September, Edward Mutch of Belleville, with a bid of $18,000, was awarded the contract for construction of the building, and on November 13, the cornerstone was laid. On August 15, 1914, with 4,500 books on the shelves, the library was opened to the public.

Nutley's first ambulance, purchased in 1911, was a combination ambulance and patrol wagon pulled by a team of horses and manned by the five officers of the police department. As the population of the town grew and the number of medical emergencies increased, a group of volunteers organized themselves to provide the necessary services to the town. The Nutley Volunteer Emergency Rescue Squad is shown here on its first day of operation on May 9, 1953. Since its inception, the squad's numbers have increased to 4 career members, 60 volunteer members, 4 ambulances, 1 rescue truck, 2 boats, 1 dive trailer, and 5 bicycles. They purchased the building at 119 Chestnut Street in 1963, and after renovations, it became their headquarters in 1964. In 1976, an addition was built to the west side of the building to house the rescue truck. The squad responds to between 3,000 and 3,500 calls per year, approximately 250 of which are mutual aid calls to neighboring communities. They not only respond to medical emergencies but also work closely with the fire department in responding to rescue duties, such as confined space rescues, high angle rope rescue, and vehicle extrication. They are a nonprofit organization that serves township residents at no charge. The year 2003 marks 50 years of providing the highest quality of emergency medical service to the township of Nutley.

In 1851, Henry Stager donated the property at 65 Church Street for the purpose of a school. It took two years for the town to build a frame school on the land. In the winter of 1874, the building caught fire and burned down. In 1875, a brick schoolhouse was built, and classes were held there until 1894, when they were transferred to the newly erected Park School. The Church Street School was used as an overflow school until 1910, when it became a boys' vocational school. In 1927, the school was disbanded and the building was used by various town organizations as a meeting place. In 1946, the building was leased to the Nutley Historical Society. The second floor of the building serves as a museum for the preservation and dissemination of Nutley's history. The picture below

shows an auction being held in front of the building. The trim above the door and the window were the first use of tan brickwork in this area. It is because of this unique design, and the significance of the building to the history of Nutley, that the building is listed on the National Register of Historic Places.

Ann Troy, principal of Washington School and one of the founders in 1945 of the Nutley Historical Society, was essential in creating a museum "to collect, preserve, and diffuse such information as may be available in the field of genealogy connected with the town of Nutley [and] include the collection of historic objects, museum materials, copies of local papers, old Church records, private papers, monographs, letters, and other materials of such nature." The society continues to uphold these objectives today. Troy would often conduct museum tours for the schoolchildren in town. This tradition has continued throughout the years, and tours are still conducted each spring for classes in the elementary schools in town.

In the 1800s, the people of Franklin were dependent upon the mills and the quarries to make a living. The Duncans owned vast holdings and ran several mills within the town. In 1852, William Duncan began building the Essex Mills in this building located on Chestnut Street, which is now the town hall. William's son Henry B. Duncan is shown standing on the right in the doorway. During the Civil War, the mills were enlarged at a cost of $75,000 as the demand for woolen blankets and blue woolens for uniforms increased. The Essex Mills had 28 looms that were all steam operated. During the war years, employees were generously paid $5 to $7 per week for six 12-hour days. When the war ended, the mill returned to, among other things, the production of green coverings for billiard tables and paisley shawls, which

Chapter 3

BUSINESSES

were rated the best made in this country. In 1884, the administration of Grover Cleveland lowered the tariffs against imported woolens, and the mill's business declined steadily thereafter.

The Park Market, shown here in 1934, was located on Franklin Avenue near the corner of Church Street. The business would continue to grow with the town and eventually moved farther north on Franklin Avenue, becoming the Nutley Park Shop Rite. As you can see, the businesses have changed and the buildings have been updated, but architecturally they remain the same.

This *c.* 1900 photograph shows the building located at 338 Passaic Avenue. At that time, Thomas Hayes, who was a plumber and gas fitter, owned the business. Hayes's business rapidly grew as more and more people opted for indoor plumbing. Loving care was taken to restore this building, which is now a restaurant called Papillon.

The southeast corner of Centre Street and Franklin Avenue was a bustling area in the early 1900s. The Great Atlantic & Pacific Tea Company is the first store on the left in the picture above. The trolley had two lines that ran through Nutley. One ran from Irvington to Nutley, and the other ran from Newark through Nutley to Paterson. Although the mode of transportation has changed dramatically, the building looks very much the same as it did 100 years ago.

The Nutley Train Station, located at Highfield Lane and Whitford Avenue, was a very busy place during the late 1800s and early 1900s. Nutley was a weekend retreat for many New Yorkers who would use the train to commute back and forth. Annie Oakley and Mark Twain were only a few of the many well-known people who visited Nutley often. They were regular patrons of this train station and of Guthrie's Store, which was only a half block west of the railroad station. Although the railroad station is no longer standing, the tracks are still used daily for freight trains.

UTLEY RAILROAD STATION, NUTLEY, N. J.

With the Stirratt livery stable just east of Passaic Avenue on Chestnut Street, it follows that the blacksmith shop would not be far away. The Yereance Blacksmith Shop was located only a few blocks west on Chestnut Street, where the Elks building now stands. From left to right are Bertram Yereance, Samuel Hopper (grandfather of Wilson Keirsted), ? Harris (a former slave), and three unidentified gentlemen.

Franklin Avenue and High Street was a very busy area during the early 1900s. Not only was the West Nutley Train Station, located on High Street near the corner of Franklin Avenue, used daily for commuters to and from New York, but the trolley that ran along Franklin Avenue was also popular for more local commutes. The building shown below housed the Masonic Temple, the Great Atlantic & Pacific Tea Company (on the right), and Murad (on the corner), advertised as the "the Daddy of Them All," which sold prescriptions, drugs, films, ice cream, candy, and Coca-Cola. On the left of the building was one of the U.S. Stores. Although the train station is no longer standing, this intersection of town is still a very busy business district.

West Nutley Station - Nutley N.J.

269-C

Wm. A. Lambert - Architect

The West Nutley Train Station was very active in the early 20th century, with passenger trains running daily and filled with commuters who worked in New York City but preferred to live in a more suburban setting. With the increasing popularity of motor vehicles, however, passenger train use began to decline. Finally, the line began to be used exclusively for freight purposes. The station was subsequently demolished, and the property was sold for commercial use.

Located in the center of the business district at the time, the Lefferts owned the first drugstore in Nutley. On the corner of Passaic and Nutley Avenues, it was less than two blocks from the Nutley Train Station on Highfield Lane. Shown here are Myrtle C. Leffert, her father, and her aunt Emma.

The *Nutley Sun* building was located at 475 Franklin Avenue near the corner of Vreeland Avenue. Previously known as the *Rising Sun*, it was purchased by William Taylor and was enlarged and improved in 1894. J.D. Foy was assigned the interests of the paper by Taylor and proceeded to make the *Nutley Sun* the "Legal Paper of the Town of Nutley." Under his ownership, it became quite successful. It changed owners and locations several times since then and is still being published today, with the offices now located at 90 Centre Street.

In the early 1900s, the building located at the corner of Park Avenue and Weston Street housed businesses that would handle all of your apparel-repair needs. On the left side of the entrance door, the window reads, "Park Avenue Shoe Repairing Shop," and underneath was the name A. Algieri. A smaller pane of glass advertised, "Repairing While U Wait," under which was a picture of shoe, and under the shoe was printed "SHINE INSIDE." On the right side of the door was the Park Avenue Ladies-Gents Custom Tailor Shop. It seems that the street name was destined to be part of the business titles for merchants at that location, and today the business at that corner is the Park Avenue Haircutting Studio. Although the original building and the business located in the small store

to its left have been replaced with a more modern commercial structure, the house on the left of the picture remains the same.

The corner of Passaic Avenue and Chestnut Street was at one time considered the center of town. Many businesses were located in this area. Stirratt's Livery was just to the east on Chestnut Street. Leffert's Drug Store was a short block north on Passaic Avenue, and Thomas Hayes Plumbing was on the northeast corner. Its proximity to the railroad station on Highfield Lane made it very convenient for commuters to do shopping, conduct business, or rent a horse and carriage. Although still a business area, Franklin Avenue has now become the main business district in the town.

Dr. Satterthwaite owned the Columbia Building, located to the east of Guthrie's Store at 288-290 Highfield Lane. This building housed stores on the first floor and apartments on the second floor. In 1898, Dr. Satterthwaite gave one of the rooms to the Nutley Library to temporarily move the library from a small building opposite the railroad station. The library remained at the Columbia Building for almost two years and was then returned to its original location. It remained there until 1904, when it was moved to 381 Passaic Avenue.

The LoCurcio family began the Park
Market in 1932 at 303 Franklin
Avenue. They remained at that location
for 11 years until their business outgrew
its humble beginnings. In 1953, they
opened a much larger store farther north
on the street at 411 Franklin Avenue. It
had an expanded inventory and came to
be known as Park Foods. During their
time at this location, the LoCurcios
partnered themselves with Thomas

Infusino and became the Nutley Park
Shop Rite. Again, in 1963, the business
outgrew the building and moved farther
north to 437 Franklin Avenue. The store
expanded yet again at this location in
an effort to provide continued service
to the town. The owners of the Nutley
Park Shop Rite have always been very
community minded and have contributed
generously to different organizations
within the township. In times of public
emergencies or crisis, they are always
on hand to donate food and supplies to
police, fire, or rescue squad personnel
who may have to spend prolonged
lengths of time on emergency duty.

Nutley's first bank was established in June 1906. Although incorporated on November 15, 1905, the first corporate meeting was not held until June 5, 1906, in the town hall. The new Bank of Nutley offered many services, and, in 1910, outgrew its original simple quarters. A new building was erected at the corner of Chestnut Street and Vincent Place and housed the bank until 1926. Various businesses have occupied the building since, and it is currently an ophthalmologist's office.

Bank of Nutley, Nutley, N

Wilson O. Davis began business in 1897. W.O., as he was usually called, sold shoes and other dry goods in the store. The store, located at 350 Passaic Avenue, was originally a one-story building, but Davis added a second and third floor soon after he took ownership. Annie Oakley was a regular visitor of the Davis Dry Goods Store. She would often use the safe that Davis kept in the rear of his building. Davis enlarged his store to accommodate a window-shade business that his son John Milton Davis had started in 1918. The business was very successful, and the building still houses the Davis-Taylor Shade Shop.

This church, located at 66 Passaic Avenue, was founded on February 8, 1937. The only member at the time was the Reverend Moon, who was the pastor of the church. Reverend Moon worked very hard to increase his congregation, which by 1942 had reached 12 members. Although the congregation itself only numbered 12 worshippers, the Sunday school department had an enrollment of 45 boys and girls.

Chapter 4

HOUSES OF WORSHIP

The Protestant Reformed Dutch Church of Franklin, better known today as Franklin Reformed Church, was organized on May 6, 1855. Sebastian Duncan served as the first senior elder and was also the clerk. Services and Sunday school were held in a building provided by John W. Stitt. In 1859, Stitt intimated that the lease on his building would soon expire, and in January 1860, the congregation arranged to use Public School No. 5 at the top of Church Street. Henry Stager had already donated land across the street from the Church Street School, as Public School No. 5 was more commonly known, with the stipulation that a church would be erected and part of the property would be used as a cemetery. The cornerstone for the building was laid in April 1861. As the congregation grew, the need for additional space was met with the erection of the parish house in 1921.

St. Mary's Church was originally dedicated as Our Lady of Grace. William Joyce, an Episcopalian and owner of the Avondale quarries, donated the land for the church. Concerned about the religious needs of the Irish and Italian quarrymen who worked for her husband, Elizabeth Joyce contacted Hubert DeBurgh of St. Peters' Church in Belleville. Pastor DeBurgh had been an Episcopal minister who converted to Catholicism, and he agreed to help establish a new church for the quarrymen. On September 22, 1872, the cornerstone of the brownstone church was laid, but the building was not completed until December 1876. The congregation continued to increase steadily until the church could no longer hold all those who tried to attend. In 1926, the old church was abandoned for the new and

larger church directly across the street. Eventually, the old church was demolished and replaced with a parking lot.

Built in the mid-1700s, this house was used as the parsonage for the Methodist church that was built next to it *c.* 1830. The church was a plain one-room building, and the property around the church and parsonage was used as a cemetery. It remained in use as a church and Sunday school until a larger building was erected in a more central location on Vincent Place. Vincent Methodist Church is located there today.

In the early 1900s, the congregation of the Methodist church located on Passaic Avenue began making plans for a new church that would be larger and more centrally located. On January 6, 1909, ground was broken at the site of the dismantled Woolen Mills on Elm Street (now Vincent Place) for the new Vincent Methodist Church. Bishop Neely laid the cornerstone on April 3, 1909, and Bishop Vincent dedicated the church on Sunday, January 2, 1910. In 1928, with the rapidly growing congregation, it was decided to enlarge the building. In February 1929, plans were adopted to add a three-story education building, including a chapel.

More than 125 years ago, Episcopalian families would travel by boat via the Passaic River to attend services at Christ Church in Belleville. In the winter months, the long commute became increasingly difficult for families with young children, so an Episcopal Sunday school was established in a laundry building owned by Thomas W. Satterthwaite in 1863. The Sunday school moved two more times after that—once to a storefront on Passaic Avenue and then to the Passaic Avenue School. The growing number of Episcopalians in Franklin would lead Satterthwaite to donate a parcel of land at the corner of Grant and Whitford Avenues for a church to be built. On Easter Sunday in 1873, the first service of Grace Episcopal Church in Franklin was held.

Originally located on the northeast corner of Grant and Whitford Avenues, Grace Church soon outgrew its small wooden frame. The property on Highfield Lane that had been donated in 1891 for the construction of a church rectory was very large, and in 1908, the decision was made to build a larger church adjacent to the rectory. The new church and parish hall were constructed of brownstone from the Nutley quarry at a cost of $30,000. The first service in the new church was held on Christmas morning in 1908. Clinton Balmer, a well-established painter, was commissioned to paint 12 murals depicting scenes from the Bible to cover both sides of the church ceiling and both sides of the east window. Balmer spent from 1910 to 1917 producing the murals, which were dedicated in June 1918. On December 30, 1925, a fire ravaged the roof and organ in the church. All of the murals except those flanking the east window were destroyed. Renovations on the church were completed on June 6, 1926. Balmer had read about the fire in the newspaper and offered to replace the murals at minimal cost. The second set of murals took from 1926 to 1929 to complete.

Grace Church, Nutley, N. J.

On March 18, 1894, a group of Nutley residents gathered at the home of Walter J. Roberts to discuss the possibility of organizing a Congregational church. Other meetings followed, and in April, St. Paul's Congregational Church was founded. Between then and February 1898, while plans were being made to build a church, services were held in two private homes. A site on the northern end of Franklin Avenue was chosen, and the church was built. The dedication services were held on February 9, 1898, and the Sunday service was held on February 13.

Yantacaw Lake was located in
Yantacaw Park between Vincent
Place and Booth Drive. After a young boy
drowned there, the lake was filled in. It is
now just a stream that is part of the Third
River, which runs through Nutley.

Chapter 5

PARKLAND

Yanticaw Park Lake, Nutley, N. J.

This is the entrance to the Nutley Park section of town during the late 1800s. William A. Lambert, an architect and builder, was responsible for the construction of the many of the homes in this area of town in the late 1800s and early 1900s. This picture shows Passaic Avenue at the intersection of Brookfield Avenue with narrow dirt roads. Although the streets have been widened and paved and the trees have grown significantly, many of the homes remain as they were 100 years ago, and the stone pillars still mark the entrance to this section of town.

This *c.* 1900 view looks south from the bridge on Brookfield Avenue. Other than the retaining walls and the bridges that now cross the stream, this parkland has remained much the same. Erie Place can be seen on the right. The Nutley Train Station was located only a few blocks to the southeast, and the railroad trestle in the center of the picture, although not visible in the current picture, is still in use on a daily basis for freight trains.

This *c.* 1892 photograph shows the Nutley Water Works and Cotton Mill Pond. The building to the right covered a large spring of clear, pure water that was pumped to limited water mains from the pumping station nearby. James R. Hay, on whose large estate the plant was located, founded the Nutley Water Company. In 1896, the township of Franklin purchased the whole system at a cost of $47,000. At that time, there were only 172 consumers, and the total budget of the water department was $1,341. In the foreground, Cotton Mill Pond furnished power for a cotton mill near Vreeland Avenue and is now known as the Mud Hole.

From 1666, when Capt. Robert Treat purchased the Passaic River valley from the Native Americans, the river has always played an important role in the development of the area. Before rail travel was available, the river served as a means of travel and transported goods and raw materials. In the mid-to-late 1800s, the *Passaic Queen* steamed up and down the river, making two round trips daily ferrying passengers between Newark and Passaic. There was a dock at the foot of Grant Avenue from which Duncan's Mills shipped all its woolen goods. Also, brownstone from the Nutley quarry was put on barges docked by the Avondale Bridge and taken to New York to build the famous brownstone mansions.

ERIE R.R. BRIDGE
NUTLEY, N.J.

The Passaic Avenue trestle has been a fixture in Nutley since the trains were first introduced into the area. The Nutley Train Station was one block southeast from this point. Passaic Avenue and Chestnut Street, located only a few blocks south, were the center of the business district in the late 1800s. Just north of the trestle was the Nutley Park section of town, where William Lambert built many homes in the late 1800s and early 1900s. To the right of the trestle were homes, and to the left was parkland, which has remained so and is now Memorial Park.

This is a picture from *c.* 1902. Records indicate that there has been a school in existence in Nutley since as early as 1794. Many schools have been built in different areas of Nutley over the years to accommodate the growing number of families. From the time of the Passaic Avenue School and the Church Street School, both built in the mid–1800s, the town has understood the need for the quality education of its children. As the town grew, so did the number of public schools. Nutley now has five public elementary schools for kindergarten through grade 6, a middle school for grades 7 and 8, and a high school for grades 9 through 12.

Chapter 6

SCHOOLS AND STUDENTS

B uilt in 1926 as the Nutley High School, it remained as such until 1959. At that time, the high school housed grades 10 through 12. On the other side of Franklin Avenue, the junior high school housed grades 7 through 9. With increasing enrollment, the schools were rapidly becoming too small to accommodate the number of students. An addition was made to the junior high school, and plans were made to redistribute the classes within the two schools. When the students returned from summer vacation in September 1959, the high school had become the junior high school (housing grades 7 and 8), and the newly enlarged junior high school had become the high school (housing grades 9 through 12). The junior high school was subsequently renamed the Franklin Middle School.

The Park Oval is located on Franklin Avenue adjacent to the high school and directly across the street from the Franklin Middle School. The field, which now contains a football field and baseball diamond, has been used for sporting events, physical education classes, high school and middle school graduation exercises, as well as various town activities. Shown in the picture below is a tug of war that took place in January 1918. As you can see, sleigh riding was also a popular winter sport. The town hall is on the left of the picture, and the Vincent Methodist Church can be seen in the background.

Spring Garden School was built in 1917 to accommodate the increasing student population in the elementary schools. Only 10 years later, in 1927, the school had to be expanded to meet the growing need for more classrooms. Classes continued to grow and become overcrowded until a fifth elementary school, located between Lincoln and Spring Garden Schools on Bloomfield Avenue, was built.

Records show that the first school in the area was in existence as early as 1794. It was located in what was called the Lower District, at the corner of Passaic Avenue and Avondale Road (which would later be renamed Park Avenue), and was known as the Old Stone Schoolhouse. The school was built on land donated by John K. Spear. The building was replaced by the Passaic Avenue School *c.* 1850, also known as the Avondale School or Little White School. The school was in use for approximately 50 years. The site on which the school once stood is now an empty lot.

In the mid-to-late 1800s, with the quarries located in the southeast section of town and the mills using the river to transport goods, the Avondale section of town began to increase greatly in population. Families remained in this area even after the quarries were closed and abandoned. Washington School was built at 155 Washington Avenue in 1911 to accommodate the increasing number of students in this section of town. An addition was made to the school in 1927 when expanding enrollment began to overcrowd the classrooms.

William Lambert rapidly built houses to the east of Passaic Avenue in the Nutley Park section, on land that had once been part of the Satterthwaite estate. With the dramatic increase in homes in this area, the need for a new school became evident. The same year that Franklin changed its name to Nutley, in 1902, Yantacaw School was built on the west side of Passaic Avenue. It was a period of rapid growth within the town, and an addition was made to the school in 1929 to help alleviate the overcrowding within the classrooms.

In 1890, the township of Franklin purchased Duncan's Essex Woolen Mills, consisting of 12 acres of land and several abandoned structures. Several buildings were demolished, but the Duncan homestead (the library site) and the mill (the town hall) were retained and used for school classes. In 1894, to the south of the homestead, the first unit of the Park School was built with additions in 1907 and 1922. In 1956, the 1894 and 1922 sections were removed and a new addition was made to accommodate the junior high school, which housed grades seven through nine. In 1959, in order to better serve the students, the junior high school and the high school traded names and redistributed the classes.

During the late 1940s and early 1950s, the population of the township of Nutley was exploding with Baby Boomers. By the early 1950s, it became evident that Lincoln School, on Harrison Street, and Spring Garden School, on South Spring Garden Avenue, were becoming increasingly overcrowded with more and more children enrolling for kindergarten each year. It was decided that a fifth elementary school would be built between the two existing schools at 379 Bloomfield Avenue. Radcliffe School—named for Paul Radcliffe, who was superintendent of schools from 1920 to 1934—opened its doors in September 1955. Over the next several years, enrollment continued to increase, and in 1967, an addition was made to the back of the school. In August 1982, when enrollment began to decrease, the Nutley Board of Education relocated its offices to the south end of the building.

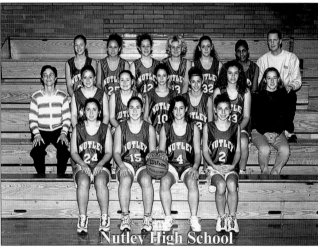

In the early 1900s, girls wanting to participate in team sports in high school had a very limited choice. Shown here is the 1909 girls' basketball team, consisting of 15 young women, and their coach. Female students now have more options than did their counterparts in the early 1900s, and basketball continues to be a very popular sport. Oddly enough, the current varsity girls' basketball team still consists of 15 players.

As with most high schools, sports play an integral part of student activities. In 1909, the football team included 13 players and 1 coach. The teams have increased in number as the game has evolved over the last 92 years. The 2001 varsity football team now boasts a 53-member team and a coaching staff of 6. The current picture was taken at the north end of the Park Oval. Note that the brick building behind the team was where the Yereance Blacksmith Shop was located in the late 1800s.

PHOTO BY
G.H. STACEY
NUTLEY

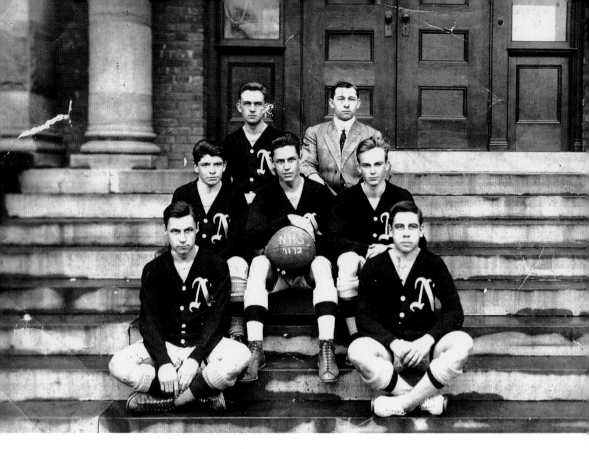

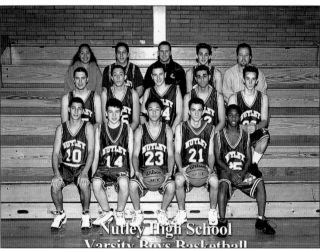

The 1911–1912 Park High School boys' basketball team consisted of six players and one coach. With so few players, absences for any reason left the team with no backup at all. The absence of more than one player would mean disqualification from competition with another school. Twelve players of the 2001–2002 team are shown to the left in the school gymnasium.

Baseball has always been America's pastime, and it certainly has been a much-loved part of Nutley's history. In 1913, with a team of 11 players and 1 coach, the interschool games would bring out many spectators to cheer their hometown team on. The 2000–2001 baseball team consisted of 15 players and 3 coaches. Baseball still draws many fans who enjoy the game and the opportunity to root for the home team and support the students.

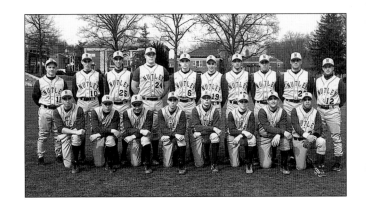

In 1915, with Nutley's population numbering approximately 7,000 residents, the graduating class shown sitting on the front steps of Park School numbered 20 students. Since that time, the population of Nutley has quadrupled, and the town has grown and prospered without losing its sense of community. On the steps of the Park Oval, adjacent to the high school, 253 students of the Nutley High School graduating class of 2001 are ready to embark on the next phase of their lives. These young women and men are the future of our world and our community; we hope that once they have completed their education they, as many of their family before them, will decide to continue to make Nutley their home. It is hoped that they, their children, and their grandchildren will maintain, preserve, and keep the integrity of our town's rich history throughout Nutley's next 100 years, as their parents, grandparents, and past generations have done before them.